Our Favorite
Grilling
recipes

Copyright 2015, Gooseberry Patch
Previously published under ISBN 978-1-93189-087-8

Cover: Beef Fajita Skewers (page 25)

Grilling Tips & Tricks

- Choose the right temperature for the food you're grilling. If you can hold your hand 6 inches above the coals for 4 seconds, it's MEDIUM...for 2 seconds, it's HOT!

- Medium heat is best for grilling chicken, pork, sausages and thick fish fillets...it will cook thoroughly without burning.

- Select high heat for steak, shrimp and thin fish fillets...it will sear the outside and form a nice crust without overcooking the center.

- An instant-read meat thermometer is handy to check doneness. Medium-rare steaks should be 145 degrees, pork or burgers 160 degrees, and chicken breasts 165 degrees.

- Use tongs or a spatula to turn the meat, not a fork which will cause tasty juices to escape and meat to toughen.

- Cooking in aluminum foil is a fun way to prepare all-in-one meals. Be sure to select heavy-duty aluminum foil...and watch out for escaping hot steam when you open the package!

- Many of these recipes can be prepared on a countertop grill, oven broiler or a stovetop ridged grill pan. Foil packages can be popped right in the oven. Give it a try!

Brush the grill rack with oil or give it a spritz of non-stick vegetable spray...foods won't stick and clean-up is easier.

Country-Style BBQ Sauce

Makes about 3 cups

1/2 c. onion, chopped
1 T. oil
1 c. catsup
3/4 c. water

1/3 c. vinegar
1/2 c. brown sugar, packed
1 t. Worcestershire sauce
1/4 t. celery seed

In a saucepan over medium heat, sauté onion in oil until tender.
Blend in remaining ingredients. Reduce heat; simmer for 20 minutes,
or until sauce thickens. Brush sauce over chicken or ribs during last
few minutes of grilling.

Before marinating chicken or chops, pour some marinade into
a plastic squeeze bottle for easy basting...how clever!

Hawaiian Pork Chops

6 pork chops
20-oz. can pineapple slices,
    drained and 1/4 c. juice
    reserved
1/2 c. soy sauce

1/3 c. oil
1/4 c. onion, minced
1 clove garlic, minced
1 T. brown sugar, packed

Place pork chops in a large shallow dish; set aside. Combine reserved pineapple juice, soy sauce, oil, onion, garlic and brown sugar, mixing well. Pour over pork chops; cover and refrigerate for at least 2 hours. Remove pork chops, reserving marinade. Grill over medium coals for 4 to 5 minutes per side, turning frequently and basting with marinade. Top each chop with a pineapple slice during last 5 minutes of grilling.

Burgers don't have to be ordinary! Ground turkey, chicken or even ground sausage are all scrumptious. Season with seasoning blends found at the meat counter like Italian, Mexican, Southwest or Mediterranean...yum!

Garlic & Mustard Burgers

Makes 4 servings

1 lb. ground beef
3 T. country-style Dijon mustard
5 cloves garlic, chopped
14-oz. jar roasted red peppers,
    drained

4 slices Monterey Jack cheese
4 hamburger buns, split

Mix ground beef, mustard and garlic well; form into 4 patties about
3/4-inch thick. Grill, covered, for 12 to 15 minutes, turning once.
Top with roasted peppers and cheese slices during last few minutes
of grilling. Place burgers on buns to serve.

Traveling a distance to your cookout site? Wrap and freeze burgers or marinated meat before packing in an ice chest. The frozen meat will help keep other items cold and will thaw in time for grilling.

Chuck Wagon Dinner

Makes 4 servings

1 lb. ground beef
1 onion, chopped
2 potatoes, sliced
2 carrots, peeled and sliced
1 green pepper, diced

1 stalk celery, diced
14-1/2 oz. can diced tomatoes,
    drained
seasoned salt and pepper
    to taste

Form beef into 4 patties; place each patty on a large sheet of aluminum foil. Top patties with vegetables in order given. Sprinkle with seasoned salt and pepper. Bring ends of foil together and roll tightly; fold ends to seal. Grill on outer edges of coals for about 20 to 30 minutes, turning occasionally. Open carefully, allowing hot steam to escape.

Hosting a barbecue will guarantee a big turnout of friends & neighbors! Load grills with chicken, ribs, brats, burgers and hot dogs, then ask guests to bring a favorite side dish or dessert to share. Add a game of softball and it's a winner!

Savory Pork Chops

Makes 6 servings

6 pork chops
3/4 c. soy sauce
1/4 c. lemon juice

1 T. chili sauce
1 T. brown sugar, packed
1/4 t. garlic powder

Place pork chops in a large plastic zipping bag; set aside. Mix together remaining ingredients; set aside and refrigerate 1/4 cup for basting. Pour remaining marinade over chops; shake to coat. Refrigerate for 3 hours to overnight. Drain and discard marinade. Grill chops, covered, for 4 minutes; turn and baste with reserved marinade. Grill for an additional 4 to 7 minutes, until juices run clear.

Soak wooden kabob skewers in water at least 20 minutes
before using...they won't burn or stick.

Skewered Scallops

Makes 4 servings

2 T. lime juice
1 T. oil
1 clove garlic, pressed
1/2 t. ground cumin

1/8 t. cayenne pepper
1 lb. sea scallops
2 c. cherry tomatoes

Whisk together lime juice, oil, garlic and spices in a small bowl; set aside. Thread scallops and tomatoes alternately onto skewers; place in a shallow dish. Brush with marinade; cover and refrigerate for 30 minutes. Grill for 5 to 7 minutes, turning and basting occasionally.

Turn an old wheelbarrow into a grill! Insulate it with 6 inches
of gravel or sand and cover with heavy aluminum foil.
Top with charcoal...a grill that goes anywhere!

Zesty BBQ Shrimp

Makes 4 to 6 servings

1 c. cider vinegar
1/2 c. catsup
2 T. brown sugar, packed
1 T. red pepper flakes

1 t. hot pepper sauce
1 t. onion powder
salt and pepper to taste
24 to 36 medium shrimp

Combine all ingredients except shrimp in a one-pint glass jar. Shake well; refrigerate sauce for at least 24 hours. Thread shrimp onto skewers. Grill for 2 to 3 minutes on each side, brushing generously with sauce.

Tie up a bunch of fragrant herbs like rosemary, oregano or thyme with jute to use as a basting brush while grilling.

Grilled Greek Chicken

Makes 4 to 6 servings

4 to 5 lbs. chicken
1 c. water
1/4 c. olive oil

5 lemons, divided
2 T. dried oregano
salt and pepper to taste

Place chicken in a large bowl; set aside. Combine water, oil, juice of one lemon and oregano; drizzle over chicken. Halve remaining lemons; squeeze over chicken. Cover bowl with a damp cloth and refrigerate overnight. Preheat grill to medium-low; brush with oil to prevent sticking. Arrange chicken on grill; turn every 10 minutes, basting occasionally with extra marinade. Grill for about 40 minutes, until juices run clear. Sprinkle with salt and pepper to taste.

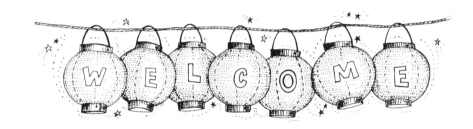

String up twinkly white lights and brightly colored
paper lanterns in the backyard...so festive!

Yippie-Yi-Yo Chile Beef Ribs

Makes 4 servings

3 to 4 lbs. beef back ribs,
    trimmed and cut into
    serving-size portions
1-1/2 t. salt
1 t. pepper
4-oz. can diced green chiles,
    drained

1 onion, minced
1 clove garlic, minced
1/2 c. honey
1/2 c. catsup
1 T. chili powder
1/2 t. dry mustard

Sprinkle ribs with salt and pepper; rub into surface. Arrange ribs on a medium-hot grill; cover and grill until tender, about one to 1-1/4 hours, adding more coals as needed. Combine remaining ingredients in a small saucepan; simmer over low heat for 10 minutes. Baste ribs with sauce during last 30 minutes of grilling, turning often.

Burgers are even more mouthwatering when served on toasty grilled buns! Simply place buns split-side down on the grill for one to 2 minutes, until golden.

Blue Cheese Burgers

3 lbs. ground beef
4-oz. container crumbled
    blue cheese
1/2 c. fresh chives, minced
1 t. Worcestershire sauce

1/4 t. hot pepper sauce
1 t. dry mustard
1-1/2 t. salt
1 t. pepper
12 hamburger buns, split

Combine all ingredients except buns in a large bowl; mix well.
Cover and refrigerate for at least 2 hours. Form into 12 patties;
grill over high heat to desired doneness, turning to cook on both
sides. Serve on buns.

Have a kabob buffet and let your guests make their own.
Set out bowls full of sauces, cubed meats, fruits
and veggies and watch the skewers fill up!

Beef Fajita Skewers

Makes 8 servings

1 lb. boneless beef top sirloin,
    sliced into 1-inch cubes
8 wooden skewers, soaked
    in water
2 onions, cut into wedges
1 green pepper, cut into wedges

1 red or yellow pepper,
    cut into wedges
2 onions, cut into wedges
3 T. lime juice
1/3 c. Italian salad dressing
salt to taste

Thread beef cubes onto 4 skewers; thread peppers and onions onto remaining skewers. Combine lime juice and salad dressing; brush over skewers. Grill over hot coals or on a medium-hot grill, turning occasionally, 7 to 9 minutes for beef and 12 to 15 minutes for vegetables. Sprinkle with salt to taste.

A clean grill makes the tastiest foods. If there's no wire brush handy, simply use balls of crumpled aluminum foil as scouring pads to clean the racks of your grill.

Honeyed Broilers

2-1/2 to 3-lb. chicken,
   quartered
4 cloves garlic, minced
1-1/2 t. dried marjoram
1 t. dry mustard

1/4 t. salt
1/4 t. pepper
2 T. honey
2 T. balsamic vinegar

Remove and discard skin from chicken quarters, if desired; arrange in a shallow dish and set aside. Mix garlic and seasonings; rub into chicken. Combine honey and vinegar; brush over chicken. Cover and chill for at least 2 hours. Place chicken, bone-side down, over medium heat on grill rack above drip pan. Cover and grill for 50 minutes to one hour, until juices run clear.

New terra cotta pots make great serving dishes or ice buckets! Just line them with plastic before using.

Smoky Sausage & Veggies

Makes 3 to 4 servings

1-1/2 lbs. green beans, trimmed
1 lb. redskin potatoes, quartered
1 to 2 sweet onions, sliced
1-1/2 lbs. smoked sausage,
    sliced 1-inch thick

1 t. salt
1 t. pepper
1 T. butter, sliced
1/2 c. water

Arrange green beans, potatoes and onions on a large sheet of aluminum foil; top with sausage. Add salt and pepper; dot with butter. Bring up foil around ingredients; sprinkle with water and close tightly. Place packet on a hot grill; cook for 30 to 45 minutes, turning once, until sausage is browned and vegetables are tender. Open carefully, allowing hot steam to escape.

An old-fashioned barrel can become a clever trash bin for your next get-together...so much nicer than metal or plastic! Remember to tuck in a plastic liner to protect it.

Grilled Ham Steak

1/4 c. apricot preserves
1 T. mustard
1 t. lemon juice

1/8 t. cinnamon
2-lb. ham steak

Blend together preserves, mustard, lemon juice and cinnamon in a small saucepan. Cook over low heat, stirring constantly, until thoroughly combined, about 3 minutes. Set aside. Grill ham steak over medium heat for 8 to 10 minutes per side. Brush with glaze during last few minutes of grilling. Slice into portions for serving.

Freeze chicken breasts or pork chops with their marinades
in airtight containers. By the time it's thawed for cooking,
the meat will have absorbed just enough flavor...so easy!

Crispy Lemon Chicken

Makes 4 to 6 servings

2-1/2 to 3 lbs. boneless,
    skinless chicken breasts
1 c. oil
3/4 c. lemon juice
1 T. seasoned salt

2 t. paprika
2 t. onion powder
2 t. dried basil
2 t. dried thyme
1/2 t. garlic powder

Place chicken in a shallow pan; set aside. Combine remaining ingredients in a jar. Cover and shake to blend; pour over chicken. Cover and refrigerate for several hours to overnight, turning several times. Grill chicken over hot coals for 15 to 20 minutes, turning frequently, until juices run clear, basting often with marinade.

Look beyond traditional napkins when hosting family & friends.
Try using bandannas, colorful tea towels, inexpensive fabrics
from a craft store, or for especially saucy foods,
use moistened washcloths...they'll love it!

34

Rib Shack Baby Back Ribs

Makes 2 to 4 servings

1-1/2 lbs. baby back pork ribs,
    trimmed and cut into
    serving-size portions
2 T. oil
1 onion, chopped
1 stalk celery, chopped

1 clove garlic, minced
1 c. catsup
1/4 c. brown sugar, packed
2 T. Worcestershire sauce
1 T. Dijon mustard

Bring a large pot of water to a boil; add ribs and simmer, covered, for about 20 minutes. Drain ribs; pat dry with paper towels and set aside. Heat oil in a saucepan over low heat; add onion, celery and garlic. Sauté until tender, about 5 minutes. Add remaining ingredients; simmer for about 10 minutes. Pour sauce into a food processor or blender; blend until smooth and let cool slightly. Brush ribs generously with sauce; grill over hot coals for 5 to 6 minutes. Turn ribs; brush again with sauce and grill for an additional 6 minutes. Bring any remaining sauce to a boil; serve with ribs.

Fill fajitas with grilled vegetables and cheese
for a satisfying lighter meal.

Sirloin & Veggie Fajitas

Makes 6 to 8 servings

1 lb. beef sirloin steak
3/4 c. salsa
2 T. olive oil
2 T. lime juice
2 cloves garlic, minced
Optional: 2 T. tequila
2 red or yellow peppers, halved

4 slices red onion
1 zucchini, sliced lengthwise
1 yellow squash, sliced
   lengthwise
8 7-inch flour tortillas, warmed
1 c. shredded Mexican-blend
   cheese

Combine steak, salsa, oil, lime juice, garlic and tequila, if using, in a large plastic zipping bag. Seal bag and turn to coat steak; add vegetables and turn to coat. Refrigerate at least 2 hours. Remove meat and vegetables from bag, reserving marinade; grill both for about 5 minutes per side, or until meat is medium-rare. Thinly slice meat and vegetables; arrange over warmed tortillas. Heat remaining marinade to a boil; drizzle over top. Sprinkle with cheese and roll up.

Cookouts can have a whimsical theme to make decorating more fun! Choose something easy that everyone will enjoy...a beach party, fiesta or western barbecue would all be terrific.

Key Lime Chicken

Makes 4 servings

4 boneless, skinless
   chicken breasts
3 T. soy sauce
1 T. honey

1 T. olive oil
2 T. lime juice
3 cloves garlic, minced

Place chicken in a large plastic zipping bag; set aside. Mix remaining ingredients in a small bowl; pour over chicken. Refrigerate for one hour; discard marinade. Grill chicken on a medium-hot grill for about 10 to 15 minutes per side, until juices run clear.

Throw a picnic night at home! Just toss a checkered tablecloth on the dinner table and set out paper plates and disposable plastic utensils. Relax and enjoy dinner...no dishes to wash!

Hip-Hip Hooray Hot Dog Sauce *Makes 4 to 6 servings*

1 lb. ground beef
1/4 c. onion, chopped
1/8 c. green pepper, chopped
1 c. catsup
1/4 t. salt
1/4 t. pepper

1/4 t. garlic powder
1/4 t. chili powder
1/8 t. cinnamon
1/8 t. red pepper flakes
6 hot dogs
6 hot dog buns, split

Combine beef, onion and green pepper in a skillet over medium heat. Cook until beef is browned and vegetables are tender. Drain. Stir in remaining ingredients; simmer over low heat for about 30 minutes. Grill hot dogs as desired; place in buns and top with warm sauce.

It's so easy to make grilled quesadillas to suit your taste!
Cooked chicken, sautéed red pepper strips and zucchini slices,
even sweet corn kernels are all scrumptious.
Quesadillas make tasty appetizers too!

Sweet Onion Quesadillas

Makes 3 to 6 servings

1 to 2 sweet onions, sliced
1 T. butter
6 8-inch flour tortillas, divided

8-oz. pkg. shredded Mexican-
    blend cheese
Garnish: sour cream

Sauté onions in butter over medium heat until tender and golden. Spoon onto 3 tortillas; sprinkle with cheese. Top with remaining tortillas. Place quesadillas on a medium-hot grill; cook until lightly golden on bottom. Turn over carefully; cook until golden on other side. Remove from grill and cut into wedges. Serve with sour cream.

Vintage carry-alls are terrific for corraling clutter. Pick up a few to use in the kitchen, or on a backyard buffet table.

Stacie's Grilled Pizza

Makes 8 to 10 servings

2 c. water
1-1/2 T. active dry yeast
1 T. sugar
3 c. bread flour, divided

1 T. salt
3 c. all-purpose flour, divided
1 T. olive oil
Garnish: desired pizza toppings

Heat water until very warm, about 115 degrees. In a large bowl, sprinkle yeast and sugar over water; stir to combine. Let stand until foamy, about 10 minutes. Add 2 cups bread flour and salt; whisk hard for 3 minutes, until smooth. Add remaining bread flour and 2-3/4 cups all-purpose flour, 1/2 cup at a time, stirring with a wooden spoon. Turn out onto a floured surface. Knead until soft, about 5 minutes, adding remaining flour one tablespoon at a time. Place in a greased deep bowl; turn once to coat. Cover with plastic wrap; let rise in a cool area until triple in bulk, 1-1/2 to 2 hours. Turn out onto a floured surface. Divide into 4 portions; roll out 1/4-inch thick. Drizzle with oil; place on hot grill. Grill 5 minutes; turn over. Garnish as desired; grill until bottom is golden and toppings are warmed.

Sing songs around the campfire. Who cares if everyone's off key? It's a fun way to make the best memories!

Campout Beef Stew

Makes 4 servings

1 lb. stew beef, cubed
4 potatoes, peeled and cubed
8 carrots, peeled and sliced
4 onions, chopped

4 cloves garlic, minced
salt and pepper to taste
4 T. water
4 T. butter, sliced

Divide beef cubes and vegetables among 4 large sheets of aluminum foil. Sprinkle with garlic, salt, pepper and water; dot with butter. Bring together edges of aluminum foil and seal tightly. Place on a heated grill or bury in campfire coals until meat is tender, about one hour. Open carefully, allowing hot steam to escape.

Hosting a backyard gathering? Fill a child's little red wagon with ice and tuck in bottles of soda and lemonade. Use colorful ribbon to tie a bottle opener to the handle so it stays near the drinks.

Chuck Wagon Chops

Makes 4 to 6 servings

6 bone-in pork chops
salt and pepper to taste
1 T. all-purpose flour
1/2 c. barbecue sauce

1 onion, thinly sliced
4 potatoes, peeled and sliced
1 T. oil
2 t. chili powder

Arrange pork chops without overlapping on a large sheet of aluminum foil. Add salt and pepper to taste. Stir flour into barbecue sauce; spoon over pork chops. Arrange onion slices over top. Toss together potatoes, oil and chili powder; arrange in an even layer over onion slices. Seal foil package tightly. Place on grill; cover and cook over medium-high heat for 25 to 30 minutes. Open carefully, allowing hot steam to escape.

Keep flying insects out of picnic beverages...just stitch
4 large beads or buttons to the corners of a table
napkin and drape over an open pitcher.

Brats & Sauerkraut

Makes 6 servings

2 T. vinegar
1/4 c. sugar
1 c. sauerkraut, drained and
    coarsely chopped
2 T. onion, diced

2 T. green pepper, diced
1 T. pimento, diced
6 bratwurst
6 hard rolls, split and toasted
Optional: coarse mustard

Combine vinegar and sugar in a small saucepan; bring to a boil, stirring until sugar dissolves. Combine sauerkraut, onion, green pepper and pimento; stir into vinegar mixture. Simmer until onion and pepper are tender; keep warm. Place bratwurst on a charcoal grill 3 to 4 inches from coals. Cook for 20 to 25 minutes, turning occasionally, until cooked through. Drain sauerkraut mixture; spoon over bratwurst on toasted rolls. Serve with mustard, if desired.

Sprinkle dried herbs like tarragon, rosemary, oregano or sage over hot coals before grilling...they'll enhance the flavor of the food.

Sweet Italian Sausage Patties *Makes 8 to 10 servings*

2 lbs. ground pork
1 T. dried parsley
2 t. garlic powder
2 t. paprika
2 t. salt
1-1/2 t. fennel seed

1/2 t. pepper
1/8 t. dried thyme
1/8 t. nutmeg
1/4 t. allspice
1/4 t. ground bay leaf
8 to 10 hamburger buns, split

Combine all ingredients except buns; mix well. Form into 8 to 10 patties; grill until cooked through, turning once. Serve on buns.

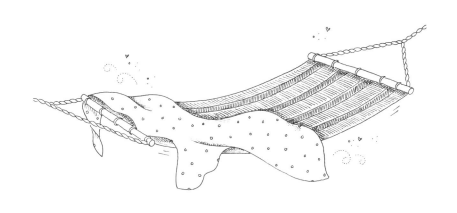

Grilling means summertime fun...pick up some squirt guns
or small battery-operated fans to keep everyone cool.

Red-Hot Pork Chops

Makes 4 servings

4 boneless pork chops
1/2 c. orange juice
3 T. brown sugar, packed
1 T. lemon-garlic seasoning

1/4 t. cayenne pepper
1/2 t. red pepper flakes
1 T. oil

Place pork chops in a large plastic zipping bag; set aside. Combine remaining ingredients; mix well and sprinkle over chops. Seal bag and refrigerate for 30 minutes to overnight. Remove chops from bag; discard marinade. Grill for 7 to 9 minutes per side, until juices run clear.

Spread lettuce leaves on hot coals before grilling juicy steaks.
The lettuce won't burn and the leaves will catch dripping fats.

Sweet-Hot Ribeye Steaks

Serves 4 to 6

2 1-lb. boneless beef
   ribeye steaks
2 cloves garlic, pressed
2 t. water

2 T. sweet-hot mustard
1 t. fresh rosemary, chopped
salt and pepper to taste
1/2 t. fresh thyme, chopped

Place steaks in a shallow dish; set aside. Combine garlic and water
in a microwave-safe dish; microwave on high setting for 30 seconds.
Blend in mustard and seasonings; stir well. Brush sauce on both sides
of steaks. Grill over coals to desired doneness, about 12 minutes for
medium. Slice into portions for serving.

Woe to the cook whose sauce has no sting.

-Geoffrey Chaucer

Zingy Chile Chicken

Makes 4 servings

4 boneless, skinless chicken
    breasts
salt and pepper to taste
3/4 c. chili sauce

2 T. oil
2 T. lemon juice
2 cloves garlic, minced
3 T. fresh basil, chopped

Sprinkle chicken with salt and pepper to taste; set aside. Blend remaining ingredients in a small bowl. Grill chicken on a medium-hot grill, turning and brushing with sauce every 10 minutes, for about 40 minutes, or until juices run clear.

Have star-spangled barbecues all summer long! Use red, white & blue tableware along with mini flags and sparklers in the centerpieces.

Marinated Flank Steak

Makes 4 servings

1-1/2 lbs. beef flank steak
1/2 c. soy sauce
1/4 c. red wine or beef broth
2 T. Worcestershire sauce
2 T. oil
juice of one lime

1/2 bunch green onions,
    chopped
1 clove garlic, minced
1 t. dill weed
1 t. celery seed

Place steak in a large plastic zipping bag; set aside. Combine remaining ingredients; mix well and sprinkle over steak. Seal bag and refrigerate overnight. Grill over hot coals to desired doneness (5 to 6 minutes per side for medium-rare). Remove from grill; let steak rest for 10 minutes before slicing on the diagonal.

Everyone loves a picnic and you don't need to head to
the park to have one. Even if you don't have a deck or patio,
colorful blankets spread on the lawn (or in the living room!)
create excitement for guests.

Santa Fe Pork Kabobs

Makes 4 servings

4 boneless pork chops, cubed
1-1/4 oz. pkg. taco seasoning
    mix

1 onion, cut into 1-inch squares
1 red pepper, cut into
    1-inch squares

Toss together pork cubes and seasoning to coat. Thread pork cubes, onion and pepper pieces onto skewers. Grill on a medium-hot grill until pork is browned, about 10 minutes, turning occasionally.

Bring along colorful vintage salt & pepper shakers to the next carry-in...they'll add a little whimsy!

Green Chile-Chicken Quesadillas   *Makes 8 servings*

1 lb. boneless, skinless
   chicken breasts, cubed
3 T. oil, divided
15-oz. can black beans,
   drained and rinsed
8-3/4 oz. can corn, drained
4-oz. can diced green chiles

1-1/4 oz. pkg. white chicken
   chili seasoning mix
1/4 c. water
8 8-inch flour tortillas
8-oz. pkg. shredded Mexican-
   blend cheese

Over medium-high heat, sauté chicken in one tablespoon oil until
golden. Add vegetables, seasoning mix and water; reduce heat and
simmer for 6 to 8 minutes. Spoon 1/2 cup chicken mixture and
1/4 cup cheese onto each tortilla; fold in half, pressing down lightly.
Brush outsides of tortillas lightly with remaining oil. Grill over
medium heat for 2 to 3 minutes on each side, turning carefully,
until golden and cheese melts. Cut into wedges to serve.

Paper plates and cups don't have to be plain and boring.
Look for brightly colored ones, then quickly dress them up
with ribbons, rick-rack, flowers or stickers.

Grilled Chicken Salad

Makes 4 servings

1 c. apple, peeled, cored
    and finely chopped
1/2 c. apple juice
1 T. cider vinegar
1 t. cornstarch
4 boneless, skinless chicken
    breasts

6-oz. pkg. mixed salad greens
1/2 c. red pepper, sliced
3/4 c. crumbled blue cheese
1/2 c. shredded Cheddar cheese
1/4 c. sliced almonds, toasted

Combine apple, juice, vinegar and cornstarch in a small saucepan over medium heat; cook and stir until thickened. Chill. Grill chicken breasts until juices run clear; let cool, then slice. Divide salad greens among 4 serving plates; top each with grilled chicken, red pepper and a sprinkling of cheeses and almonds. Drizzle with dressing and serve immediately.

Aluminum foil is handy when grilling fish or vegetables...it keeps foods from falling into the coals. Simply lay a length of foil over the grill and spray lightly with non-stick vegetable spray.

Salmon & Dilly Cucumber Sauce   *Makes 4 servings*

4 6-oz. salmon fillets
1 T. olive oil

1 T. lemon juice
salt and pepper to taste

Brush salmon on both sides with oil and lemon juice; sprinkle with salt and pepper. Grill over hot coals for 4 to 5 minutes on each side, turning carefully, just until fish flakes easily. Serve with sauce.

Sauce:

1 c. water
1/3 c. white vinegar
1 c. sugar
1 T. salt

1 cucumber, peeled and diced
1 c. sour cream
1 T. fresh dill, chopped

Combine water, vinegar, sugar and salt; stir until sugar dissolves. Stir in cucumber; chill for one hour. Drain, discarding liquid; fold cucumber into sour cream. Stir in dill.

For a special touch when serving seafood, wrap lemon halves in cheesecloth, tie with a colorful ribbon and set one on each plate. Guests can squeeze the lemon over their dishes... the cheesecloth prevents squirting and catches seeds!

Dijon-Grilled Fish

Makes 2 to 4 servings

1 lb. orange roughy fillets
1/2 c. butter
2 T. Dijon mustard

2 T. lemon juice
1 t. seasoned salt
Garnish: paprika

Place fish fillets in a shallow dish; set aside. Combine butter, mustard, lemon juice and salt in a small saucepan; simmer over low heat for 10 minutes. Let cool; pour over fish. Cover and refrigerate for 30 minutes. Grill over medium coals for 3 to 6 minutes on each side, basting with remaining sauce. Sprinkle with paprika.

Bottled Italian salad dressing doubles as a quick meat marinade...adds juiciness and zingy flavor!

Jamaican Marinade for Chicken *Makes one cup*

1/3 c. olive oil
3 T. white vinegar
1-1/2 T. lime juice
1 T. sugar
1/4 c. green onion, minced
1 jalapeño, seeded and
    chopped

2 cloves garlic, minced
1 t. dried thyme
3/4 t. allspice
1/2 t. cinnamon
1/2 t. salt
cayenne pepper to taste

Combine all ingredients; mix well. To use, marinate chicken in refrigerator for 2 to 3 hours before grilling.

A gift for Dad of a spatula, tongs, a basting brush and a jar
of steak rub would be terrific tucked inside an oven mitt!

Cookout Steak Rub

Makes about 1-1/2 cups

1/2 c. brown sugar, packed
1/4 c. sugar
2 T. chili powder
2 T. paprika
2 T. dry mustard
2 T. garlic powder

2 T. dried, minced onion
1 T. dried oregano
1 T. dried thyme
1 T. dried basil
1 T. cayenne pepper

Combine all ingredients; mix well. Store in an airtight container.
To use, rub generously over steaks before grilling.

Don't worry about a specific cookout menu...if friends offer to bring a dish to share, welcome it! It's always fun to see what traditional foods other families enjoy.

Pot Roast on the Grill

Makes 4 servings

2-lb. beef chuck roast
6 new potatoes, quartered
1 onion, quartered
3 carrots, peeled and sliced

8-oz. pkg. sliced mushrooms
2 stalks celery, sliced
seasoning salt and pepper
    to taste

On a very hot grill, brown roast on both sides just long enough to sear. Place roast on a large piece of aluminum foil; arrange vegetables on top. Sprinkle to taste with seasoning salt and pepper. Wrap up and seal edges tightly. Grill, covered, for 30 minutes; turn over, cover and grill an additional 30 minutes.

Lined with a tea towel, vintage cherry-picking pails make handy
potluck take-alongs for rolls, fresh fruit, napkins and silverware.

Barbecued Cheese Burgers

Makes 5 servings

2 lbs. ground beef
2 T. dried, minced onion
2 t. Worcestershire sauce
2 t. mustard
1 t. salt
1-1/2 t. pepper

1-1/2 c. shredded sharp
   Cheddar cheese
Optional: garlic butter, melted
5 hamburger buns, split
   and toasted

Thoroughly mix together ground beef, onion, sauce, mustard, salt and pepper. Form into 10 thin patties. Place 1/4 cup cheese on top of 5 patties; top each with another patty and press together to seal. Grill on a hot grill to desired doneness. For extra flavor, brush with melted garlic butter during grilling. Serve on toasted buns.

Uncertain whether to cover the grill or not? In general, cover large cuts of meat...keep the lid open for thin cuts or small pieces.

Bacon-Wrapped Burgers

Makes 6 servings

1-1/2 lbs. ground beef
3 T. catsup
3 T. water
2 T. fresh basil, chopped
1/2 t. dried rosemary

1/2 t. salt
1/4 t. pepper
6 slices bacon
6 hamburger buns, split

Combine all ingredients except bacon and buns in a large bowl; mix well. Form into 6 patties about one-inch thick. Wrap a bacon slice around each patty; fasten with a toothpick. Grill burgers to desired doneness, about 5 minutes on each side. Remove toothpicks and serve on buns.

Another tasty way to serve sweet corn...blend 1/2 cup
softened butter with one teaspoon fresh marjoram. Brush over
6 ears corn, pat husks back into place and grill as directed.

Roasting Ears with Spicy Butter *Makes 12 servings*

6 ears sweet corn in husks
2 qts. water
1/2 c. butter, softened

1 t. chili powder
1 jalapeño, seeded and minced
salt and pepper to taste

Soak ears of corn in water for several hours. Peel back husks and remove corn silk. Wrap husks back around ears and place on a hot grill. Grill for one hour, turning occasionally and letting outer husks blacken. Use hot pads to remove corn from grill. Blend butter with chili powder and jalapeño. To serve, peel back husks and brush with butter; add salt and pepper to taste.

Grill veggies on rosemary skewers for a savory change.
To make the skewers, pull off all but the top leaves from
the stem and whittle the opposite end into a point.
Slide on vegetables and grill...delicious!

Farmstand Veggie Kabobs

Makes 4 servings

1/2 c. Italian salad dressing
1 T. fresh parsley, minced
1 t. fresh basil, chopped
1/2 t. fresh chives, chopped
2 yellow squash or zucchini,
    sliced 1-inch thick

2 onions, sliced into wedges
8 cherry tomatoes
8 mushrooms
2 c. prepared rice

Combine salad dressing and herbs in a small bowl; cover and chill.
Alternate squash slices, onion wedges, tomatoes and mushrooms
evenly among 8 skewers; brush with dressing mixture, reserving
excess. Place skewers on grill rack over medium coals; grill for
15 minutes, or until vegetables are tender, turning and basting
frequently with reserved dressing mixture. To serve, place 1/2 cup
rice on each plate and top with 2 kabobs.

Everyone loves to exchange recipes at family get-togethers!
Drop a note in the mail ahead of time asking everyone to jot
theirs down and make lots of extra copies to share.

Yummy Parmesan Potatoes

Makes 6 servings

6 potatoes, peeled and
    thinly sliced
1 onion, thinly sliced
1/2 c. grated Parmesan cheese

2 cloves garlic, minced
4 T. butter, diced
1 t. seasoning salt
1/2 t. pepper

Combine all ingredients in a bowl; mix well. Spoon onto a double
length of aluminum foil; fold foil up around ingredients and seal well.
Grill, covered, over medium heat for 30 to 40 minutes, or until
potatoes are tender.

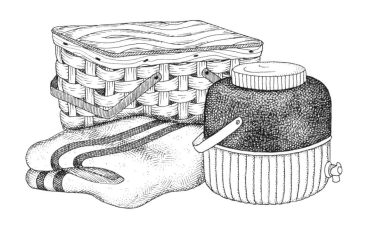

Did you know...a small bunch of mint placed in the middle of your picnic table or blanket will keep those pesky bees away?

Zesty Onion Relish

Makes about 3 cups

2 lbs. sweet onions,
   thickly sliced
1/4 c. olive oil

3 T. balsamic vinegar
2 T. brown sugar, packed
1/4 t. cayenne pepper

Lightly brush onion slices on each side with oil. Grill over low heat
for 15 minutes, or until tender and golden. Let cool; chop and set
aside in a medium bowl. Combine vinegar and brown sugar in a small
saucepan; cook and stir over low heat until sugar dissolves. Pour over
onions; sprinkle with cayenne and stir to coat. Serve warm; refrigerate
any leftovers.

Try grilling tender whole baby veggies too...delightful! Tiny eggplant, zucchini, pattypan squash, cherry tomatoes and pearl onions just need a bit of olive oil and salt before grilling.

Garden Patch Grilled Vegetables   *Makes 6 servings*

4 potatoes, sliced into wedges
6 small onions
2 to 3 carrots, peeled and
    sliced diagonally
1/2 c. olive oil
1 T. fresh thyme, chopped

1 red pepper, sliced
1 green pepper, sliced
1 zucchini, sliced
1/4 lb. sliced mushrooms
salt and pepper to taste

Combine potatoes, onions and carrots in a saucepan; cover with water and simmer until crisp-tender, about 15 to 20 minutes. Drain and let cool. Combine oil and thyme in a large bowl. Add cooked and raw vegetables; toss to coat. Arrange vegetables in a grill basket. Place on a heated grill, turning and brushing with remaining oil mixture until tender and golden. Sprinkle to taste with salt and pepper.

Vintage wire carriers are just right for toting iced tea,
napkins and flatware to the table. Look for these at flea
markets...they come in all shapes and sizes.

Grilled Herb Bread

Makes one loaf

1/2 c. butter, softened
1/2 c. grated Parmesan cheese
1 t. dried oregano
1 t. dried parsley

1 t. dried basil
1 loaf Italian bread, sliced
    1-inch thick

Blend together butter, cheese and herbs; spread on both sides of bread slices. Grill bread for 2 to 3 minutes on each side, just until golden.

Salsa isn't just for Mexican food anymore! Serve it as
a condiment with grilled chicken, steaks and even
hot dogs & burgers...delicious!

Fire-Roasted Salsa

Makes 3 to 4 cups

10 roma tomatoes, divided
8 jalapeños, divided
1/2 bunch fresh cilantro,
    minced
1 onion, chopped

6 to 10 cloves garlic, minced
1-1/2 T. lemon juice
1 T. lime juice
salt and pepper to taste

Combine 5 tomatoes and 4 jalapeños in a saucepan; cover with water and simmer for 20 to 25 minutes. Drain and chop coarsely. Arrange remaining tomatoes and jalapeños on a grill; heat until tender and slightly blackened. Remove and discard stems from jalapeños; cut into chunks. Combine tomatoes, jalapeños and remaining ingredients in a blender; blend to desired consistency, about 30 to 40 seconds. Chill and serve.

White-washed clay pots planted with herbs make
classic cookout table centerpieces.

Herbed Potato Wedges

Makes 4 servings

4 potatoes
1/4 c. fresh chives, chopped
   and divided
1 c. Italian salad dressing

1 onion, sliced
4 sprigs fresh sage
salt and pepper to taste

Slice each potato into 6 wedges. Lay 3 wedges together on a double square of aluminum foil; sprinkle with one tablespoon chives and 2 tablespoons salad dressing. Place an onion slice and a sprig of sage on remaining 3 wedges. Fit potato back together and sprinkle with an additional 2 to 3 tablespoons salad dressing. Wrap tightly. Grill, covered, over medium heat for about one hour, or until potatoes are tender. Discard sage; add salt and pepper to taste.

If someone volunteers to pitch in with get-together preparations, or offers to bring a dish, let them! Just be sure to return the favor!

Summertime Tomato Salad

Makes 6 to 8 servings

2/3 c. olive oil
1/4 c. vinegar
1 clove garlic, minced
1/2 t. salt
pepper to taste

3 T. fresh basil, chopped
1/4 c. onion, chopped
1-1/2 c. mozzarella
    cheese cubes
1 pt. cherry tomatoes, halved

Whisk together oil, vinegar, garlic, salt and pepper in a medium bowl.
Stir in basil and onion. Add cheese and tomatoes; toss to mix. Chill.

Have a bonfire weenie roast in the fall when the weather turns cool & crisp. Add a hearty pot of Boston Baked Beans, simmering spiced cider to drink and later, s'mores for dessert!

Boston Baked Beans

Makes 6 servings

2 T. brown sugar, packed
2 T. molasses
1/4 c. hot water

3/4 c. catsup
2 15-3/4 oz. cans pork & beans

Stir together brown sugar, molasses and water in a small bowl until
sugar dissolves. Stir in catsup. Pour over beans in an ungreased
1-1/2 quart casserole dish; mix well. Bake, uncovered, at 350 degrees
for one hour.

Keep 'em cool! Fill a large galvanized tub with ice, then nestle serving bowls of cold foods in the ice. Everyone can help themselves!

7-Layer Overnight Salad

Makes 8 to 10 servings

1 head lettuce, torn into
   bite-size pieces
1 to 2 onions, thinly sliced
   and separated into rings
10-oz. pkg. frozen peas

3 to 4 eggs, hard-boiled,
   peeled and sliced
4-oz. jar bacon bits
8-oz. jar mayonnaise
1-1/2 c. grated Parmesan cheese

Arrange one-third of lettuce in a large bowl. Top with one-third each
of the onions, frozen peas, eggs and bacon bits. Repeat layering twice.
Spoon mayonnaise completely over top; sprinkle with Parmesan.
Cover and refrigerate overnight.

Place packets of flower seeds in a basket by your front
door...let guests pick their favorites to take home.
As the flowers bloom, friends will be reminded of you.

Garlic Deviled Eggs

Makes 12 servings

6 eggs, hard-boiled and peeled
1/3 c. mayonnaise
1/2 to 1 t. mustard
1 t. pickle relish

1 onion, chopped
1 clove garlic, minced
1/8 t. salt
Garnish: paprika

Slice eggs in half lengthwise; remove yolks, setting aside egg whites.
In a mixing bowl, mash yolks with a fork. Add remaining ingredients
except paprika; mix well. Spoon yolk mixture into egg whites;
sprinkle with paprika. Chill.

Happiness is like potato salad...when you share it
with others, it's a picnic!

-Unknown

Mom's Picnic Potato Salad

Makes 4 servings

4 to 5 new potatoes, peeled,
    boiled and diced
2 hard-boiled eggs, peeled
    and chopped

1/3 c. onion, diced
1/4 to 1/2 c. mayonnaise
1 T. mustard
salt and pepper to taste

Combine all ingredients in a large bowl; toss until potatoes are coated well. Refrigerate overnight before serving.

Make a crunchy, fresh salad fast with fewer dishes to wash!
Toss lettuce, veggies and any other toppers in a one-gallon
plastic zipping bag. Give it a shake and pour into salad bowls.

Southwest Salad Twist

Makes 4 to 6 servings

1 c. frozen corn, thawed
15-oz. can black beans, drained
   and rinsed
3 to 4 tomatoes, finely chopped

1/4 c. green onion, chopped
1/4 c. fresh cilantro, chopped
1 T. chopped green chiles
juice of 1 to 2 limes

Combine all ingredients except lime juice in a serving bowl; mix well.
Drizzle lime juice over top; stir gently. Chill.

A splash of ginger ale in orange juice makes a refreshing beverage to accompany a cookout meal. Serve in tall glasses with lots of ice...aah!

German Potato Salad

Makes 6 servings

6 to 8 new potatoes, peeled,
    boiled and thinly sliced
10 slices bacon, chopped
1 red onion, finely chopped
4 t. all-purpose flour
1 T. sugar

salt and pepper to taste
1/2 c. cider vinegar
1/2 c. water
1/4 c. fresh parsley, minced
1 t. celery seed

Place warm potato slices in a large bowl; set aside. Cook bacon until crisp in a skillet over medium heat. Add onion and cook for one minute; stir in flour, sugar, salt and pepper. Mix together vinegar and water; pour over mixture in skillet. Stir until thickened; pour over potatoes and toss gently. Stir in parsley and celery seed. Serve warm.

Keep chilled salads cold...oh-so easy! Pop a stoneware bowl into the freezer, then at serving time, spoon salad into the chilled bowl. It will stay fresh and crisp.

Artichoke Pasta Salad

Makes 8 to 10 servings

16-oz. pkg. rotini pasta,
  uncooked
7-oz. jar sliced roasted
  red peppers, drained
6-oz. jar marinated artichokes,
  drained

8-oz. jar sliced black olives,
  drained
15 slices pepperoni
1/2 lb. Cheddar cheese, cubed
salt and pepper to taste
1 T. oil

Cook pasta according to package directions until tender but not soft.
Drain and rinse in cold water; place in a large bowl. Add peppers,
artichokes, olives, pepperoni and cheese; toss gently. Add salt and
pepper to taste; stir in oil. Refrigerate for 2 to 4 hours before serving.

Napkins are a must at cookouts! Cloth napkins are so much nicer
than paper ones...make napkin rings of grapevine and hot glue
a different button or charm on each.

Country Coleslaw

Makes 6 servings

3 c. cabbage, shredded
1 c. carrot, shredded
1/2 c. whipping cream

3 T. cider vinegar
salt and pepper to taste

Toss together cabbage and carrot in a large bowl; set aside. In a small bowl, whisk cream and vinegar together. Add salt and pepper; pour over cabbage mixture and toss to coat. Chill.

Roasted over a bonfire until warmed throughout, apples are oh-so yummy dipped into warm caramel ice cream topping.

Ooey-Gooey Banana Boats

Makes 4 servings

4 bananas
6-oz. pkg. semi-sweet chocolate
    chips

10-1/2 oz. pkg. mini
    marshmallows

Pull back one section of peel on each banana; do not remove.
Cut a wedge-shaped section out of each banana; fill with chocolate
chips and marshmallows. Replace peels; wrap each banana in
aluminum foil. Heat on grill for about 6 minutes, until chips and
marshmallows are melted.

Just for fun, create a variation on the classic s'more.
How about chocolate-striped cookies and a spoonful
of peanut butter...irresistible!

Peppermint S'Mores

Makes 6 servings

6 whole graham crackers,
   broken in half

6 chocolate mint patties
12 marshmallows

Top 6 graham cracker halves with chocolate patties; set aside.
Skewer marshmallows; toast until very soft and golden over a grill
or campfire. Immediately place a marshmallow onto each patty;
top with a graham cracker and press together.

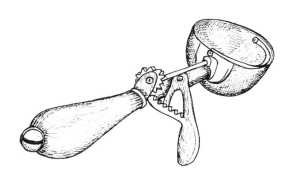

Add fun to dessert! Serve ice cream in aluminum foil-lined flower pots and add a cookie-on-a-skewer flower.

Caramelized Fruit

Makes 8 servings

1/4 c. butter, melted
1/3 c. brown sugar, packed
4 peaches, halved and pitted

8 slices pineapple
4 red plums, halved and pitted

Combine butter and brown sugar in a medium bowl; mix well. Add fruit; toss gently to coat. Arrange fruit cut-side down on a sheet of aluminum foil with edges pinched to form a rim. Place on a medium-hot grill; heat until caramelized around edges. Turn fruit and repeat, moving frequently to avoid browning. Serve warm.

Scoop out a watermelon half, then fill with juicy fresh fruit like strawberries, peaches, blueberries, bananas, grapes and watermelon balls...always a favorite!

Pineapple Sundaes

Makes 6 servings

2 T. butter, melted
1/2 c. brown sugar, packed
2 T. lemon juice
1 t. cinnamon
1 pineapple, cored, peeled and
    sliced 1-inch thick

1/2 gal. vanilla ice cream
Optional: whipped cream,
      maraschino cherries

Blend butter, brown sugar, lemon juice and cinnamon; brush over both sides of pineapple slices. Grill over high heat for about one minute per side, until golden and tender. Top each slice with a scoop of ice cream; garnish with a dollop of whipped cream and a cherry, if desired.

Bake up some cookie bars, then cut, wrap and freeze individually.
Later you can pull out just what you need for a last-minute picnic.

Sweet & Sticky S'Mores Bars

Makes 1-1/2 dozen

2 c. graham cracker crumbs
1/3 c. sugar
1/4 t. salt

1/2 c. butter, melted
3 c. semi-sweet chocolate chips
4 c. mini marshmallows

Blend together crumbs, sugar, salt and butter; set aside one cup of mixture for topping. Press remaining mixture into an ungreased 13"x9" baking pan. Bake at 350 degrees for 10 minutes, until golden. Let cool. Melt chocolate in a double boiler; spread over cooled crust. Layer with marshmallows, pressing gently into warm chocolate; top with reserved crumb mixture. Broil 2 inches from heated broiler until marshmallows are lightly golden. Let cool; cut into squares.

INDEX

INDEX

Our Story

Back in 1984, we were next-door neighbors raising our families in the little town of Delaware, Ohio. Two moms with small children, we were looking for a way to do what we loved and stay home with the kids too. We had always shared a love of home cooking and making memories with family & friends and so, after many a conversation over the backyard fence, **Gooseberry Patch** was born.

We put together our first catalog at our kitchen tables, enlisting the help of our loved ones wherever we could. From that very first mailing, we found an immediate connection with many of our customers and it wasn't long before we began receiving letters, photos and recipes from these new friends. In 1992, we put together our very first cookbook, compiled from hundreds of these recipes and, the rest, as they say, is history.

Hard to believe it's been over 30 years since those kitchen-table days! From that original little **Gooseberry Patch** family, we've grown to include an amazing group of creative folks who love cooking, decorating and creating as much as we do. Today, we're best known for our homestyle, family-friendly cookbooks, now recognized as national bestsellers.

One thing's for sure, we couldn't have done it without our friends all across the country. Each year, we're honored to turn thousands of your recipes into our collectible cookbooks. Our hope is that each book captures the stories and heart of all of you who have shared with us. Whether you've been with us since the beginning or are just discovering us, welcome to the **Gooseberry Patch** family!

Vickie & JoAnn

Want to hear the latest from **Gooseberry Patch**?
www.gooseberrypatch.com

Email

1•800•854•6673